THE LITTLE WOMEN BOOK

GAMES, RECIPES, CRAFTS, AND OTHER HOMEMADE PLEASURES

by Lucille Recht Penner
illustrated by Diane deGroat

Random House New York

Library of Congress Catalog Card Number: 94-74128 ISBN: 0-679-87405-4

Manufactured in the United States of America

10 9 8 7 6 5 4 3 2 1

Dear Reader,

Have you ever loved a book so much that you wanted to step right into it? Was it *Little Women* by Louisa May Alcott? *Little Women* is a magical book. Generations of girls have laughed and cried and dreamed over it.

The Little Women Book is a collection of activities, recipes, and games that I think would have delighted Meg, Jo, Beth, and Amy— the four sisters who live in Ms. Alcott's enchanting story.

Would you like to play games that amused the March Family? Learn how to make costumes out of scraps of silk, lace, and ribbon? Dress in gorgeous gowns, and fix your hair in ringlets or fancy braids? Set the table for fabulous parties and balls, and cook and eat delicious tea sandwiches, bonbons, and cakes?

Are you ready? Well, then, take out your favorite dress-up clothes, polish up your imagination, and prepare to enter the world of *Little Women*…

Lucille Recht Penner

CONTENTS

MARMEE'S SURPRISE

There was ice cream—actually two dishes of it, pink and white—
and cake and fruit and distracting French bonbons and,
in the middle of the table, four great bouquets of hothouse flowers!
"Is it fairies?" asked Amy.
"It's Santa Claus," said Beth.

Marmee had surprised the girls with a wonderful Christmas supper! The delicious food and beautiful flowers were a present from their neighbor, Mr. Laurence.

For a special Christmas party, create a bright bouquet of colorful flowers, make delicious French bonbons, put together a gorgeous platter of winter fruit, and enchant your guests with sparkling party crackers.

MENU
PINK AND WHITE ICE CREAM
FRENCH BONBONS
WINTER FRUIT

PINK AND WHITE ICE CREAM BALLS

ice cream scoop   *1 pint strawberry ice cream*
1 pint vanilla ice cream   *1 tray covered with wax paper*

Scoop out balls of ice cream. Put them on the wax paper–covered tray, keeping each flavor separate. Freeze for 1 hour or more.

When it's time to eat, pile the strawberry ice cream balls in one pretty dish, and the vanilla ice cream balls in another.

FRENCH BONBONS

½ cup butter, softened

¼ cup heavy cream

½ teaspoon almond food flavoring

1 lb. confectioners' sugar

6 drops red food coloring

½ cup granulated sugar

Beat the butter. Beat in the confectioners' sugar. Stir in the cream, food coloring, and almond flavoring.

Dip your fingers into granulated sugar so the dough won't stick to them. Shape teaspoonfuls of dough into balls. Roll each ball in sugar.

Put the balls on a sheet of wax paper and let them harden in the refrigerator for 1 hour or more.

Makes four dozen bonbons.

WINTER FRUIT

Arrange apples, pears, pomegranates, tangerines, dates, and figs on a large platter. Surround the fruit with a circle of evergreens and pine cones.

HOTHOUSE FLOWERS

colored tissue paper, cut into 8-inch squares   *perfume*
green pipe cleaners

To make each flower, pile up eight layers of tissue paper. Starting at one end, fold them up accordion-style.

Fasten the folded tissues in the middle with a pipe cleaner. Then pull up the "petals" carefully one by one.

Spray your bouquet lightly with perfume and arrange it in a pretty vase or basket.

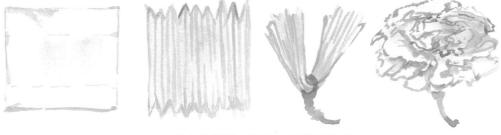

PARTY CRACKERS

cardboard toilet-paper tubes   *wrapped candies*
little presents   *bright, new pennies*
shredded paper   *colored tissue paper*
ribbons

Fill the tubes with wrapped candies, little presents, bright, new pennies, and shredded paper. Then wrap the tubes in colored tissue paper, twist the ends, and tie them with pretty ribbons. Decorate the crackers with glitter glue, green and red star-shaped stickers, or little pictures cut out of magazines and catalogs.

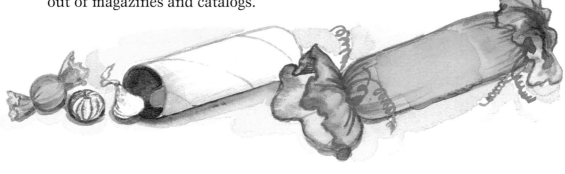

GIVING IS SWEET

"She's coming! Strike up, Beth! Open the door, Amy!
Three cheers for Marmee!" cried Jo,
prancing about while Meg went to conduct Mother
to the seat of honor.

Meg, Jo, Beth, and Amy loved to give presents to each other and to their mother. They always made a great ceremony out of presenting even the littlest gifts.

The girls made most of their gifts out of simple materials that they found at home. Try making these wonderful surprises for your family and friends.

SEASHELL HEART BOX

small seashells (or shell-shaped pasta)   *white glue*
a small covered cardboard box

Draw a heart on the cover of the box. Then carefully squeeze and spread glue inside the heart. Stick on shells or pasta. Let it dry overnight.

FRIENDSHIP PILLOW

pieces of pretty cotton fabric   *needle and thread*

cotton batting   *dried lavender*

embroidery silk, fabric markers, or puff paint

Cut two 3-inch squares out of different-colored fabrics. Then cut a 3 x 6–inch rectangle out of a third color.

Sew the two squares together, like this:

Open them up. Ask an adult to press the seam for you.

Sew the squares to the rectangle, leaving a small opening. Turn the pillow inside out. Fill it with cotton batting and a handful of dried lavender. Carefully sew up the opening with small stitches.

Now embroider or write on one square, "To (the name of your friend)." On the other square write, "From (your name and the year)."

You might also want to draw a flower, a star, or a little animal.

What a nice token of your friendship!

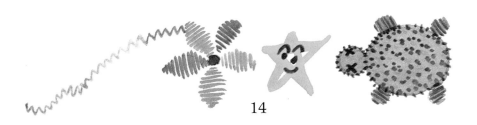

SILHOUETTE PORTRAIT

Tape a piece of paper on the wall. Shine a bright light on it. Have your subject stand between the light and the wall. Her shadow will fall on the paper. If she's close to the paper, her shadow will be small. If she moves far away, it will be big.

Trace around the edge of her shadow with a pencil. Then take the paper off the wall. Cut out the silhouette and paste it on a piece of colored paper.

Write the date and your friend's name on the back.

PRESSED FLOWERS

Buy or gather your favorite fresh flowers.

Spread a pile of newspaper on the floor. Place the flowers on top, leaving a small space between each one. Then cover them with more newspaper.

If your mother agrees, put the flowers and newspaper under your mattress, or cover them with a pile of heavy books.

Change the newspaper every day, until no more moisture seeps into it from the flowers. This will take about a week. Then arrange and glue the dried flowers onto a piece of paper.

Put the dried-flower picture in a pretty frame.

RIBBON FANS

11 x 5–inch paper　　　　*markers*

staples　　　　*a piece of shiny ribbon 14 inches long*

Draw a pretty design on the paper with markers. Fold the paper accordion-style, starting at a short end.

Open the paper and cut small diamond-shaped holes on each fold 1 inch from the top. Thread ribbon through the slits and make a knot at each end. Curl the ends of the ribbon.

Refold the fan and staple the bottom. Gently open the top.

When you're finished, it will look like this:

BETH'S DOLLS

Beth loved all six of her dolls. She took special care of one that was very old and ragged.

She brought it bits of bouquets…sang it lullabies, and never went to bed without kissing its dirty face, and whispering tenderly, "I hope you'll have a good night, my poor dear."

It's easy to make some of your own dolls. All you will need are tassels or yarn and bits of cloth, wool, silk, ribbons, and buttons. If you're in a great hurry, just follow the directions for making an Instant Doll.

HANDKERCHIEF DOLL

1 white handkerchief   *white thread*
wool   *sequins or beads*

Spread out the handkerchief. Gently lift it and tie a small "head" in the center, like this:

Sew some pieces of wool on the head to make hair. Then glue or sew sequins or beads on the doll's skirt.

TASSEL DOLL

yarn or ready-made tassel   *felt*

If you are making your own tassels, wind the yarn around your hand. Tie the top and cut the bottom. Tie off the arms and leave the rest of the yarn hanging down for a skirt. Or divide and tie the rest of the yarn to make legs.

Cut out tiny pieces of felt and glue them to the head to make the doll's eyes, nose, mouth, and hair.

AN INSTANT DOLL

Cut a doll shape out of heavy cardboard. It can be big or little. Now cut a picture of a face out of an old catalog or magazine. Paste the face on your cardboard cutout. Cut out a dress for your doll from the magazine, colored paper, or even a thin piece of fabric. Glue it onto the cutout. Your Instant Doll is ready.

A SEWING BEE

Beth loved music, but the March family was too poor to afford a piano. One day, to Beth's great joy, Mr. Laurence invited her to play his piano whenever she liked. To express her heartfelt thanks, she got busy making him a pair of slippers.

Beth worked away early and late.
She was a nimble little needle woman....

A SEWING BASKET

Everyone who sews should have her own sewing basket. It's a very special and personal item. You may use it your whole life, so you'll want to make it a lovely one. All you will need are a basket, a piece of pretty fabric, ribbons, and silk flowers.

a small covered basket with handle	*glue*
pretty fabric	*ribbon*
silk flowers	

Take the cover off the basket. To make the fabric lining, cut two pieces of fabric to fit inside the basket and the cover. Hem the edges and glue the material in place.

Weave pieces of ribbon through the basket and tie them in little bows. Twist the stems of the silk flowers through the handle.

Now you are ready to stock your basket. You will need:

spools of thread   *needles*   *pins*   *buttons*
a pincushion   *scissors*   *a thimble*

When your basket is finished, invite some friends to join you for a Doll's Clothes Sewing Bee. To make doll dresses, fold small pieces of fabric in half. Cut out holes for the neck, like this:

Put a dress over your doll's head. Now you're ready to decorate it. You can make it simple or fancy. Here are some ideas:

Use a piece of ribbon to make a pretty belt.

Sew or glue sequins onto the dress.

Make a shawl out of a scrap of lace.

String beads to make doll-sized necklaces and bracelets.

Sew on little pearl buttons.

Draw a design on the dress with fabric marker, glitter pen, or puff paint.

THE DRESS-UP BOX

Jo was always writing plays and skits for the girls to perform at home. They didn't have enough money to buy costumes, so they made them themselves. What did they make?

...Gorgeous robes of old cotton, glittering with tin spangles from a pickle factory, and armor covered with the same useful diamond-shaped bits left in sheets when the lids of tin preserve pots were cut out...

Use an old trunk or a strong cardboard box for your dress-up clothes. Ask your parents if you may put in some of their old clothes, hats, shawls, vests, and gloves. Collect bits of ribbon, lace, and leftover material. Buttons, belts, sequins, feathers, artificial flowers, masks, scarves, and costume jewelry will all come in handy.

A FANCY ROBE

Measure the distance from your neck to the floor. You will need a piece of material twice as long as that.

Fold the material in half lengthwise. Cut out a hole for your head, like this:

Now decorate your robe with a belt, scarves, ribbons, lace, sequins, or feathers. When you're done playing, put it back in the Dress-Up Box. It will be fun to use again another day.

AMY TAKES TEA

*Jo obeyed…and when she had squeezed her hands into tight gloves
with three buttons and a tassel, as the last touch of elegance,
she turned to Amy with an imbecile expression…
saying meekly—"I'm perfectly miserable; but if you consider me
presentable, I'd die happy."*

Jo hated getting dressed up to go visiting, but Amy loved it. So one day they put on their best bonnets, gloves, and gowns, opened their parasols, and went calling on their neighbors. The last stop was at the home of their frightening Aunt March.

If *you* like dressing up, get out some fancy clothes from the Dress-Up Box and invite your friends to a tea party. Set a small table with a lacy cloth and pretty china. Put a jug of fresh flowers in the middle of the table.

MENU

TEA

NUT SANDWICHES

EGG FINGERS

CUCUMBER BOATS

RASPBERRY JAM TARTS

TEA

To make tea for four people, put two teabags in the pot. Ask an adult to help you pour 4 cups of boiling water over the teabags. Let the tea steep for 5 minutes. Then ask an adult to help you pour it into teacups.

If you prefer, you may fill the teapot with lemonade or cranberry juice.

TEA PLATTER

Arrange nut sandwiches, egg fingers, and cucumber boats on a platter. Decorate them with sprigs of parsley and slices of radish.

NUT SANDWICHES

4 tablespoonfuls walnuts, chopped fine   *8 slices of whole wheat bread*
¼ lb. cream cheese, softened

Cut the crusts off the bread.

Stir the chopped walnuts into the cream cheese. Spread some on a slice of bread and cover with another slice. Cut the sandwich into triangles.

Serves four.

EGG FINGERS

4 hard-boiled eggs, chopped   *4 teaspoonfuls mayonnaise*
6 teaspoonfuls sweet pickles, chopped fine   *4 slices firm white bread*

Cut the crusts off the bread. Cut each piece into four strips.

Mash the chopped eggs and mayonnaise. Stir in the chopped pickles. Spread the mixture on the bread fingers.

Serves four.

CUCUMBER BOATS

4 small cucumbers   *1 cup cottage cheese*
2 scallions, chopped fine   *salt and pepper*

Peel the cucumbers. Cut them in half lengthwise and scoop out the seeds.

Mix the cottage cheese and scallions. Add salt and pepper to taste. Fill the cucumber boats with the mixture.

Serves four.

RASPBERRY JAM TARTS

3 egg whites   *1 teaspoon vanilla*
½ teaspoon creme of tartar   *dash of salt*
¾ cup sugar   *raspberry jam*

Separate the eggs. Save the yolks for another recipe.

Beat the vanilla, tartar, and salt into the egg whites until soft peaks form. Beat in the sugar until stiff peaks form. You have made meringue.

Butter a cookie sheet and drop tablespoonfuls of the meringue onto it. Make a little well in the center of each mound with the bottom of a teaspoon.

Ask an adult to help you bake the tarts for 20 minutes at 325°. Cool. Use a spatula to put the tarts on a rack. Fill the wells with raspberry jam.

YOUR NAME GARDEN

Meg, Jo, Beth, and Amy each had a garden to grow whatever she wished, every spring. The gardens were very different!

*Meg's had roses and heliotrope, myrtle, and a little orange tree
in it. Jo's bed was never alike two seasons; this year it was to be
sunflowers, the seeds of which . . . were to feed Aunt Cockletop
and her family of chicks. Beth had old-fashioned,
fragrant flowers in her garden…and Amy had as many brilliant,
picturesque plants as would consent to blossom there.*

Try planting a special garden this spring—one that everyone will know belongs to you because it spells out your name!

Dig up the soil in a sunny spot.

Print your name on the ground with a stick in letters at least a foot high. Dig down to loosen the dirt along the lines. Sprinkle flower seeds along each line about half an inch down. Cover them lightly with soil.

Sprinkle the seeds with water. Keep them moist and keep watching. One day your name will appear in bright blossoms!

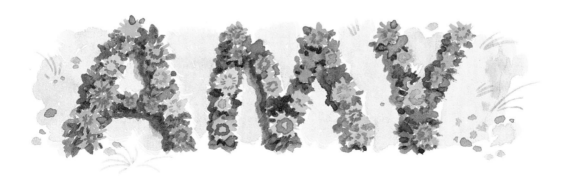

ALL SORTS OF LARKS

"Having a lark" meant having fun to the March girls and their friends. They all had great fun playing games.

They played them inside and outside, as often as they could. Here are five delightful games you can play at parties, on picnics, or any time at all.

RIGMAROLE

*"One person begins a story, any nonsense you like, and tells
as long as he pleases, only taking care to stop short
at some exciting point, when the next takes it up and does the same.
It's very funny when well done and makes a perfect jumble
of tragicomical stuff to laugh over."*

.

Would you like to try it? Have your friends sit in a circle and take turns making up one long, wonderful nonsensical tale.

GRANDMOTHER'S TRUNK

This game is most fun with at least four players.

Ask the players to sit in a circle. The first player thinks of an object. If it's a flower, she says, "I put a flower in Grandmother's Trunk."

The second player thinks of another object. If it's a ribbon, she says, "I put a flower and a ribbon in Grandmother's Trunk."

Each player continues adding something until someone makes a mistake. Then she is out. The game goes on until only one player—the winner—is left.

CHARADES

Take out your Dress-Up Box for this game. Your friends will have lots of fun putting together costumes for their charades.

Divide the players into two teams. Then divide each team into actors and guessers.

Have your team choose the title of a book and whisper it to the actors on the other team. Then the actors must dress up and act out the title for their guessers. See how long it takes them to guess it.

Then have the other team pick a title for your team to act out and guess.

The players on each team should have a chance to be actors and guessers at least once. Then, if everyone loves the game, go on playing!

TRUTH

"Do you know Truth?" asked Sallie.
"I hope so," said Meg, soberly.
"The game, I mean."
"What is it?" said Fred.
"Why, you pile up your hands, choose a number, and draw out in turn,
and the person who draws out the number has to answer truly
any questions put by the rest. It's great fun."

Some of the questions Jo and Meg and their friends asked were, "Who are your heroes?" "What is your greatest fault?" "What do you most wish for?"

Make a list of questions and gather your friends together for a searching game of Truth.

HUNT THE SLIPPER

Ask everyone to stand close together in a circle, facing inward. One player is It. She stands in the center. The children in the circle pass a slipper behind their backs. The one in the center has to guess who has it. Everyone may wiggle to make it hard to guess. When the player who is It guesses correctly, the player who has the slipper takes her place in the center.

JO AND THE HUMBLE LOBSTER

Once, when Jo tried to cook a fancy dinner, everything went wrong. She burned the bread, overcooked the asparagus, and hammered and poked at the lobster until it fell apart. But she was sure the dessert would be delicious. How could anything go wrong with strawberries and cream?

Miss Crocker tasted first, made a wry face, and drank some water
hastily....Amy...took a heaping spoonful, choked, hid her face
in her napkin, and left the table precipitately.
"Oh, what is it?" exclaimed Jo, trembling.
"Salt instead of sugar, and the cream is sour," replied Meg,
with a tragic gesture.

After a little while, everyone began to laugh and Jo felt better. But her guests were still hungry, so she quickly prepared a new dinner of bread, butter, and olives. It was a great success!

Instead of cooking a lobster, try making this pretty little meal for your friends.

MENU
BREAD AND BUTTER SANDWICHES

BLACK AND GREEN OLIVES

STRAWBERRIES AND CREAM

MILK

BREAD AND BUTTER SANDWICHES

whole wheat bread *sweet butter, softened*
black and green olives, pitted

Cut the crusts off the bread. Butter two slices for each guest. Cover each slice with another piece of bread. Cut the sandwiches into squares or triangles.

Arrange the cut sandwiches on a platter. Decorate the platter with black and green olives.

STRAWBERRIES AND CREAM

Cut the stems and leaves off the strawberries. Wash them and pat them dry. Put them in a pretty glass bowl and sprinkle them with sugar.

Fill a small pitcher with fresh cream.

When it's time to eat, set the table. Put a tall glass of milk at each place.

Pass the platter of sandwiches and olives. You can eat this part of the meal with your fingers!

For dessert, serve the strawberries and cream.

Helpful hint: *DON'T USE SALT BY MISTAKE!*

RINGLETS AND BRAIDS

Meg wanted a few curls about her face and Jo undertook
to pinch the papered locks with a pair of hot tongs.
"Ought they to smoke like that?" asked Beth from her perch on the bed.
"It's the dampness drying," replied Jo.
"What a queer smell! It's like burned feathers," observed Amy.
"There, now I'll take off the papers and you'll see a cloud of little ringlets,"
said Jo, putting down the tongs.

The girls often wore their hair in braids or curls. Here are some lovely hairstyles you can fix at home.

RINGLETS

It's easy to make pretty ringlets. Tie up your hair on top of your head with a pretty ribbon. Take small bunches of hair, moisten them with gel, and set them on rollers.

When your hair dries, take out the rollers and gently comb each bunch of hair around your finger to make ringlets.

A CROWN OF BRAIDS

Part your hair in the middle and make two braids. Fasten them with small bands. Pull one braid up and fasten it on the top of your head with hairpins the color of your hair. Pull up the other braid. Tuck the end under the first braid and pin it in place.

For a special occasion, tuck a pretty flower under one of the braids.

TOPKNOT AND CURLS

Gather your hair into a ponytail on the top of your head. Divide the ponytail into two parts. Wrap one part around clockwise and fasten it in place with pins. Wrap the second part counterclockwise and do the same.

Pull out a small lock of hair over each ear, moisten it with gel, and roll it up in a pincurl. Fasten the curl with a bobby pin. The gel will dry in a few minutes. Take out the bobby pins and gently comb out your curls.

LOOPS AND RIBBONS

Part your hair in the middle and make two braids. Bring each braid forward and stick the end through the top to make a big loop, like the picture on the left.

Tie a ribbon around it to hold the loop in place. Make a bow.

HAIR DECORATIONS

Try decorating your new hairstyles with fancy bows, tortoiseshell combs, colored ribbons, fresh or silk flowers, beads, or lacy scarves.

QUEEN FOR A DAY

The March sisters loved celebrations. On her birthday, each girl wore a crown and sat on a "throne." Beth remembered the ceremony with both fear and delight.

"I used to be so frightened when it was my turn to sit in the big chair with the crown on, and see you all come marching round to give the presents, with a kiss. I liked the things and the kisses, but it was dreadful to have you sit looking at me while I opened the bundles," said Beth.

You might like to make this ceremony a birthday tradition in your family. All you'll need to do is choose a special chair for the birthday throne and make a beautiful crown, a birthday cake, and edible necklaces.

On pages 13–17 you will find ideas for special gifts to make for the birthday person.

MENU
A CROWN CAKE

APRICOT NECTAR

RAINBOW JEWEL EDIBLE NECKLACES

THE BIRTHDAY CROWN

stiff cardboard   *silver foil*

fake jewels* or shiny paper   *glue*

Cut a 4 x 10–inch strip of stiff cardboard. Then cut it to look like the picture below.

Measure the "Queen's" head and trim the cardboard so it will fit when the ends are stapled together.

Cover the crown with silver foil.

Glue on fake jewels or circles and diamonds cut out of bits of shiny paper.

*You can buy fake jewels in the doll-making department of a crafts supply store.

A CROWN CAKE

1 yellow sheet cake   *white icing*   *pretty-colored candies*

Prepare a yellow sheet cake. Cut out a crown shape, cover it with icing, and decorate it with "jewels" made out of pretty-colored candies.

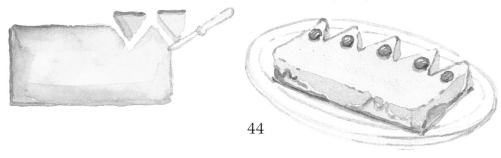

RAINBOW JEWEL EDIBLE NECKLACES

gummy worms
other brightly colored candies
needle and heavy thread

Thread the needle. String on several gummy worms and other candies in a pattern of pretty colors. They will sparkle like jewels.

Your guests will enjoy wearing their rainbow jewel edible necklaces and eating them when they get hungry.

Set the table with your prettiest dishes. Put a glass of apricot nectar and a rainbow jewel edible necklace at each place.

Pile up the presents next to the birthday person's plate.

Invite everyone to be seated, light the candles, and bring out the crown cake.

Three cheers for the Queen!